TRANSFER DESIGNS FROM AROUND THE WORLD

339 patterns to embroider or paint

KATIA FEDER & HUGUETTE KIRBY

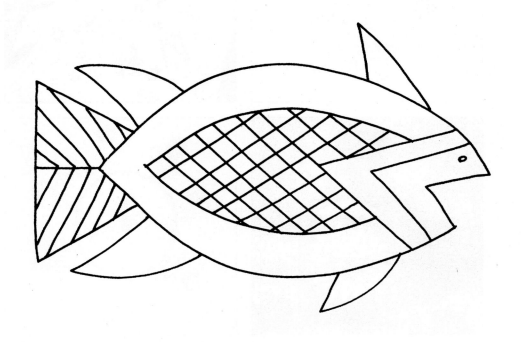

SEARCH PRESS

INTRODUCTION

This book will take you on a journey, where you can discover the rich world of decorative motifs that can be used for painting and embroidery. The patterns are taken from all five continents, where they feature in traditional and modern arts. All the designs contained in the book are transfers, suitable for use on surfaces such as fabric, paper, card and wood.

You will find the transfers in this book simple to apply and you can use them to decorate a wide range of items, including clothes and furniture. Choose from folk art patterns from Europe, or designs which have their roots in African or Indian art. There are also exciting designs originating from North and South America and the Near East. You can use coordinating designs to capture the atmosphere of a particular region or country, or you could even try mixing patterns from different cultures to create a unique flavour.

Transferring a design

The transfer patterns featured in this book can be used on paper, cardboard, wood or fabric. In this way, you can coordinate painted furniture with cushions, personalise the decor in a bedroom or even create original clothes.

Working on fabric

Transfers work well on most fabrics, although some silk and synthetic fabrics can occasionally present difficulties. Always carry out a preliminary test before you begin. Each pattern can be re-used five to eight times on thin fabrics, two to three times on thicker fabrics.

1. Cut out the chosen design.

2. Use a pencil to mark where you want the design to appear. Remember that pencil marks will disappear with washing.

3. Cover your ironing board with paper to protect it. This will prevent the design transferring on to the ironing board cover.

4. Place the item to be embroidered or painted on the paper.

5. Pin the printed side of the transfer to the fabric. Remember that the patterns shown in the book have been inverted so that they will appear the right way round once they have been transferred.

6. Place a clean sheet of paper over the transfer.

7. Adjust the iron to a non-steam cotton setting. Iron over the paper slowly, then carefully lift up a corner of the transfer to check that the pattern has been properly transferred on to the fabric.

Working on paper, cardboard or wood

Patterns can be transferred on to paper, cardboard or wood simply by ironing them on directly with a hot iron.

Note If you wish to reproduce the same pattern several times, e.g. for an all-over flower design on a tablecloth or a border around a wardrobe, transfer the design on to tracing paper first. Place the tracing face side down on your surface. Trace around the outline of the design with a ballpoint pen to transfer the design. Repeat to build up the pattern.

Repeating a pattern

A very simple design can be turned into a border or corner motif. To create a corner, place a mirror at an angle to the design and adjust until you get a right-angled image of it. Mark the angle of the mirror in pencil and then use these guide marks to transfer a repeat of the design. If you want to visualize what a design will look like repeated as a frieze, simply place a mirror vertically over it.

Embroidering

Framing up

There are lots of different embroidery frames available, including the floor frame, chair frame, slate frame, travel frame, pin frame and hoop frame. Depending on the type you use, the method of framing up will vary. However, the most important thing is to ensure that the fabric ends up drum tight. The hoop frame is very popular as it is one of the simplest frames to use. To frame up with this, place the fabric to be embroidered on the inner hoop and then force the outer hoop over the fabric to stretch it. Tighten the screw on the outer frame to secure the fabric in place. Once framed up, avoid pulling the edges of the fabric, as this may distort it.

Stitching

Centring a design: Fold the fabric into quarters, then mark a cross on the exact centre using a pencil or several tacking stitches (Diagram A). Line up the centre of the pattern with the centre of the cross.

Starting off: Choose your needle carefully, to ensure that it is not so big that it will leave holes in the fabric as you work. It is best not to make any knots in the thread but instead, start off with a number of small stitches either outside the design area, or under an area which has already been embroidered.

Simple hemming: Tablecloths, mats or serviettes, for example, are easy to hem. Allow approximately 2cm (1in) all round when cutting out the fabric. When the design is complete, mitre the corners, turn the edge under 1cm (½in) and then repeat to get a double hem (see Diagram B). Tack in place, iron thoroughly and then sew to secure.

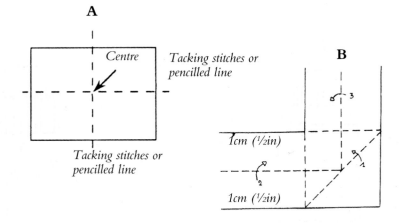

A

Centre

Tacking stitches or pencilled line

Tacking stitches or pencilled line

B

1cm (½in)

1cm (½in)

Washing and ironing a finished embroidery

1. Wash the embroidered work by hand in lukewarm, soapy water.

2. Rinse it gently, then allow to dry flat.

3. Embroidered fabric should be ironed on the reverse to avoid crushing the stitches. To do this, place the embroidered fabric face down on the ironing board. Cover with a damp cloth and press with a hot iron.

Mounting an embroidery

Once the embroidery is finished, you can stretch it over a piece of stiff cardboard or thin plywood and secure on the back with sticky tape. To cushion the embroidery or create more depth, try placing a piece of flannel underneath first. The embroidery can now be mounted and framed.

Painting on fabric

The designs in this book can be used to transform cushions, curtains, clothes and much more. It is possible to paint on to all sorts of fabrics, but generally, the thicker the fabric, the better the paint will take. Some synthetic fabrics do not take the paint very well and, of course, any fabric that cannot be ironed will not be suitable as you will be unable to fix the colours.

There are many different fabric paints on the market, all of which will produce different effects. Remember that whichever you use, the paints will fade after repeated washing. Fabric paints are acrylic-based, and most can be diluted with water. A clear medium is also available, which can be used to create soft shades.

Before you begin painting, you should first wash the fabric to remove any dirt or the manufacturer's dressing. Leave to dry and then iron it. Cover your work surface with scrap paper – this will protect your surface by absorbing any paint that seeps through the fabric. Transfer the pattern (see page 3) and then paint your design. Allow the paint to dry for several hours before ironing it on the reverse side with a hot iron to fix the colours. The fabric can now be washed gently, following the fabric paint manufacturer's instructions.

Designs can also be outlined with a special paste before painting to create a striking effect. Gutta is available from art and craft shops for this purpose. It is used as a resist when painting on fabric, particularly silk. It is supplied in a tube, and it can be piped directly on, but this may leave a thick, crude line. To obtain a fine, controlled line of gutta or fabric paint, decant it into a pipette first. Cut off the spout of the pipette (Diagram A), then unscrew the cap. Insert a 1mm (0.040in) nib into the cap (Diagram B), fill the pipette with gutta and screw the top back on. The pipette is now ready to use. Push a piece of very fine wire into the nib every time you stop work to prevent blockages (Diagram C).

Painting on wood

You can transfer a design on to wood to transform a piece of furniture or to personalise a picture or mirror frame, for example. The wooden surface should be clean and free from grease before you begin. If you are working on old wood, sand it first to remove any rough spots.

It is best to use acrylic paints on wood. These are available from art and craft shops. Acrylics are water-soluble, non-toxic, quick-drying and they offer good coverage. The paints come in a good range of colours and they can be intermixed to produce other colours, and diluted with water to create more delicate shades.

Acrylic paint is hard-wearing, but it is a good idea to apply one or two coats of acrylic varnish once the paint has dried. This will provide a tough, water- and heat-resistant finish. Alternatively, apply clear furniture wax to create a more subtle, antique finish.

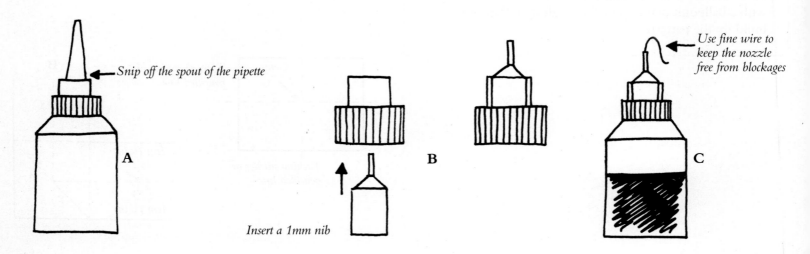

Snip off the spout of the pipette

A

Insert a 1mm nib

B

Use fine wire to keep the nozzle free from blockages

C

Embroidery stitches

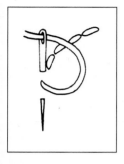

Back stitch

This is sewn from right to left, alternating with one long stitch forward and one short stitch back. This stitch is used for lines, outlines and curves.

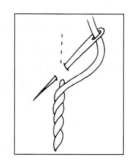

Stem stitch

Insert the needle into the fabric and bring it up half a stitch's length along from the previous stitch. The thread must stay on the same side of the needle. This stitch is used for outlines and lines. It can also be used for filling in between lines.

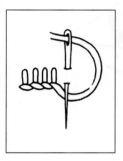

Blanket or buttonhole stitch

This stitch is sewn from left to right. Push the needle up through the fabric, then pass the thread under the needle with the help of your left thumb. Pull the stitch taut, without distorting the fabric. The stitches must be regular and close together. This is a good stitch for filling in gaps.

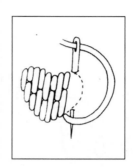

Long and short stitch

This stitch is not regular in length like satin stitch. Alternate long and short stitches as shown and use different tones of thread to create a subtle shaded effect. This stitch is used for filling in large areas.

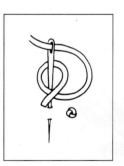

French knot

Bring the needle up where you want the knot to be positioned. Loop the thread around the needle then insert the needle close to where it first emerged. Hold the knot in place and pull the thread through. This stitch is useful for adding detail and for filling in small areas.

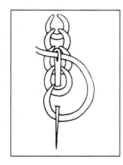

Chain stitch

Bring the needle up through the fabric, then form a small loop with the thread and hold it in place with your finger. Insert the needle back down, and then bring it up at the tip of the loop to make the next stitch. This stitch is used for outlines, borders and for filling in gaps. It can also be adapted for curves.

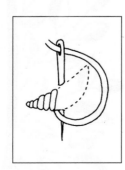

Satin stitch

This stitch can be sewn in all directions – vertically, horizontally or even in chevrons – but care must be taken to ensure that the outline is precise. Satin stitch is made up of a series of stitches, worked close together so that no fabric shows through. Try to avoid working very long stitches, as the thread may become slack. This stitch is used for filling in.

EMBROIDERY PROJECTS

The patterns shown in this section are created on linen, using two strands of embroidery thread. A small skein of each of the colours shown is sufficient for each project. Stitches and colours of thread are given, but you could experiment to create different effects. The number that accompanies each colour, refers to the DMC colour chart which is given on page 70.

Bird

Transfer Page 14, No. 42 (Oceania and Africa)

Stitches Chain stitch and satin stitch

DMC colour No. 310 (Black)

Tree

Transfer Page 14, No. 44 (Oceania and Africa)

Stitches Chain stitch and satin stitch

DMC colour No. 310 (Black)

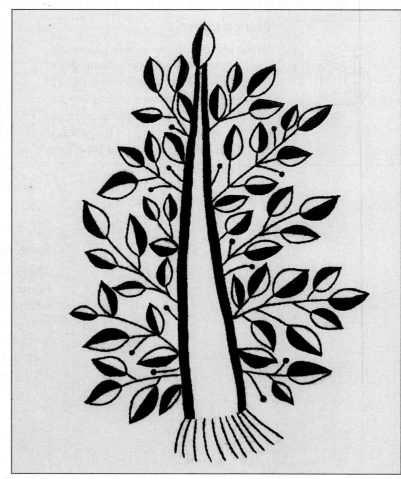

Totem pole

Transfer Page 24, No. 107 (South America)

Stitches Chain stitch and satin stitch

DMC colours No. 932 (Light Antique Blue);
No. 3047 (Light Yellow Beige); No. 921 (Copper);
No. 3777 (Very Dark Terracotta); No. 310 (Black);
No. 725 (Topaz)

Butterfly

Transfer Page 27, No. 116 (Asia)

Stitches Stem stitch and satin stitch

DMC colours No. 3350 (Medium Mustard);
No. 552 (Medium Violet); No. 211 (Light Lavender);
No. 725 (Topaz); No. 729 (Medium Golden Sand)

Flamingo

Transfer Page 35, No. 147 (Asia)

Stitches Satin stitch and long and short stitch

DMC colours No. 3047 (Light Yellow Beige);
No. 930 (Dark Antique Blue); No. 818 (Baby Pink);
No. 3354 (Light Dusty Rose); No. 961 (Dark Dusty Rose)

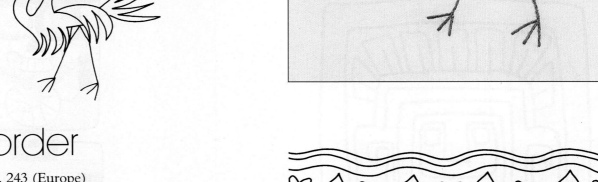

Heart border

Transfer Page 46, No. 243 (Europe)

Stitches Chain stitch and satin stitch

DMC colours No. 740 (Tangerine); No. 603 (Cerise);
No. 321 (Christmas Red)

Violet

Transfer Page 52, No. 280 (Europe)

Stitches Chain stitch and satin stitch

DMC colours No. 3777 (Very Dark Terracotta);
No. 554 (Light Violet); No. 3746 (Dark Blue Violet)

9

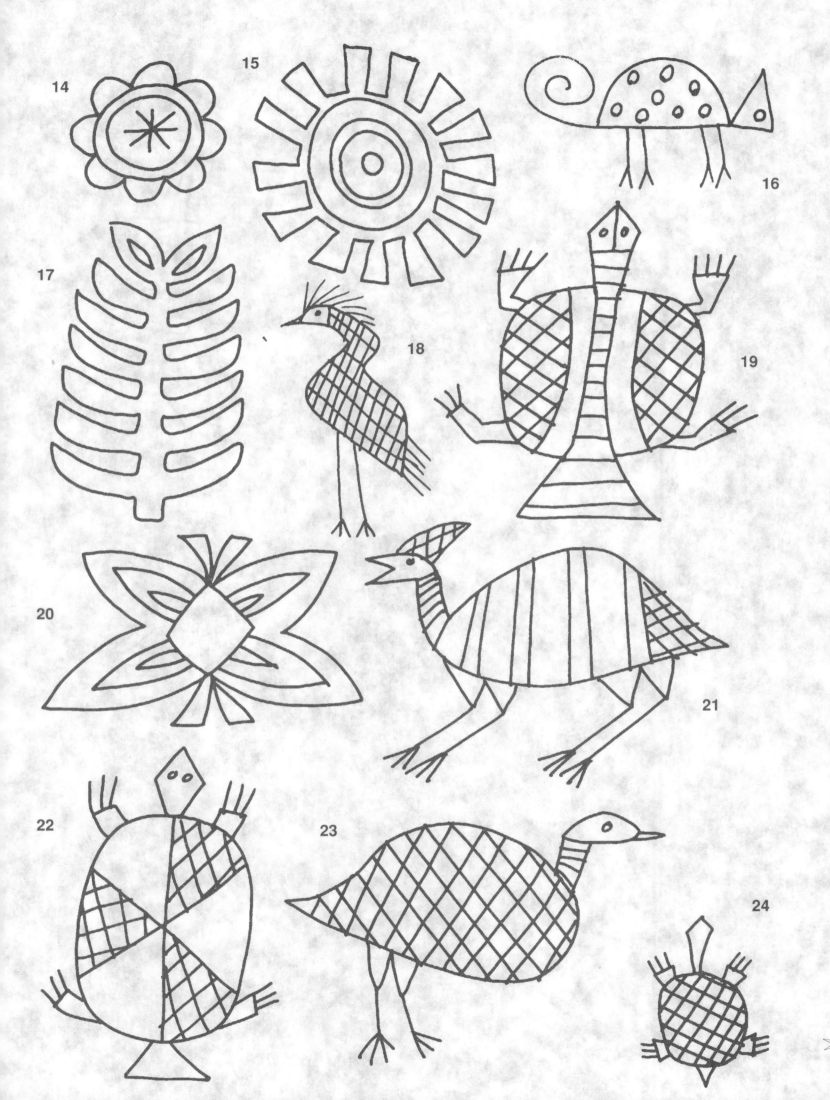

11

25

26

27

28

12

29　　　　30　　　　　　33

31

32

36

34

35

37

38

39

49   50   51   52

53

54

15

55

56

57

58

59

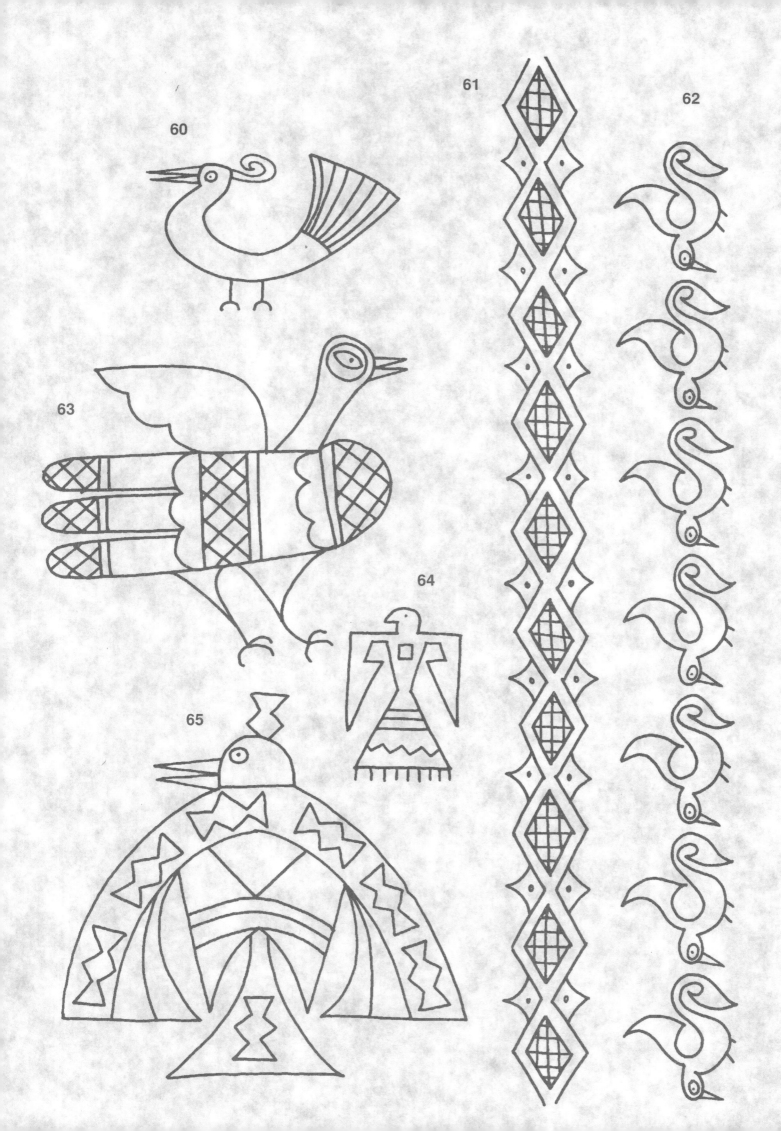

60

61

62

63

64

65

17

66

67

68

69

70

18

71

72

73

19

74

75

76

77

78

79

80

81

82

20

83

84

85

86 87

21

88
89
90
91
92
93
94
95
96
97

22

98

99

100

101

102

103

104

23

105

106

107

108

109

110

24

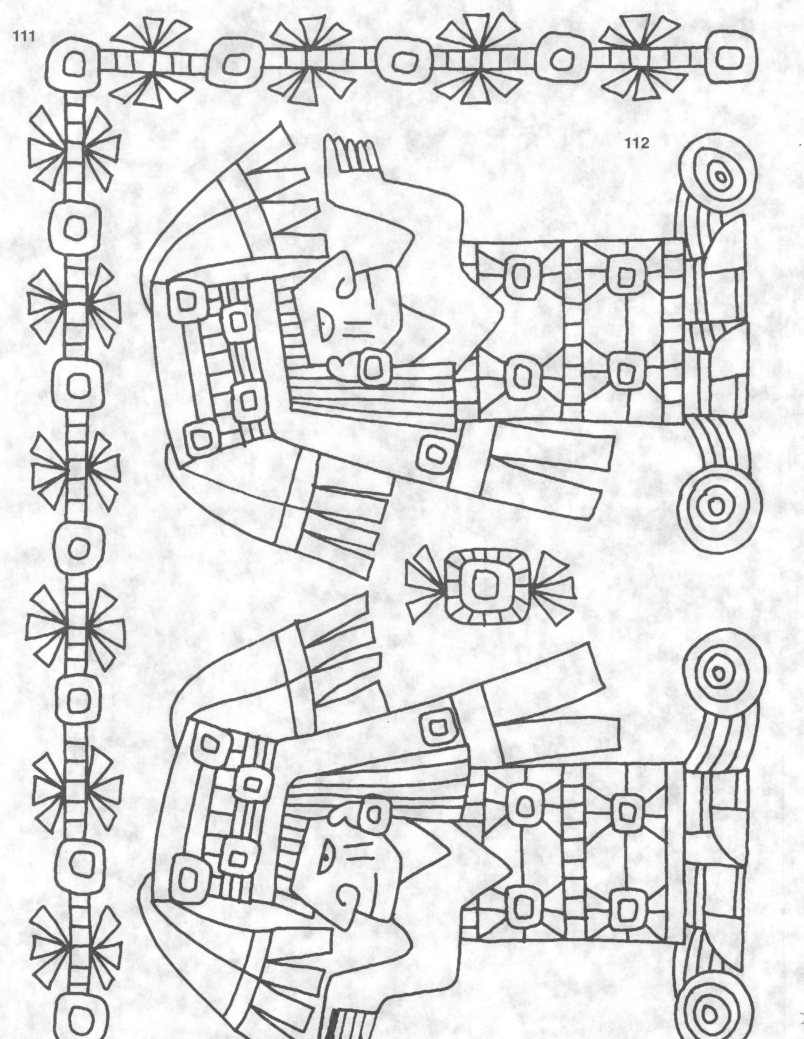

111

112

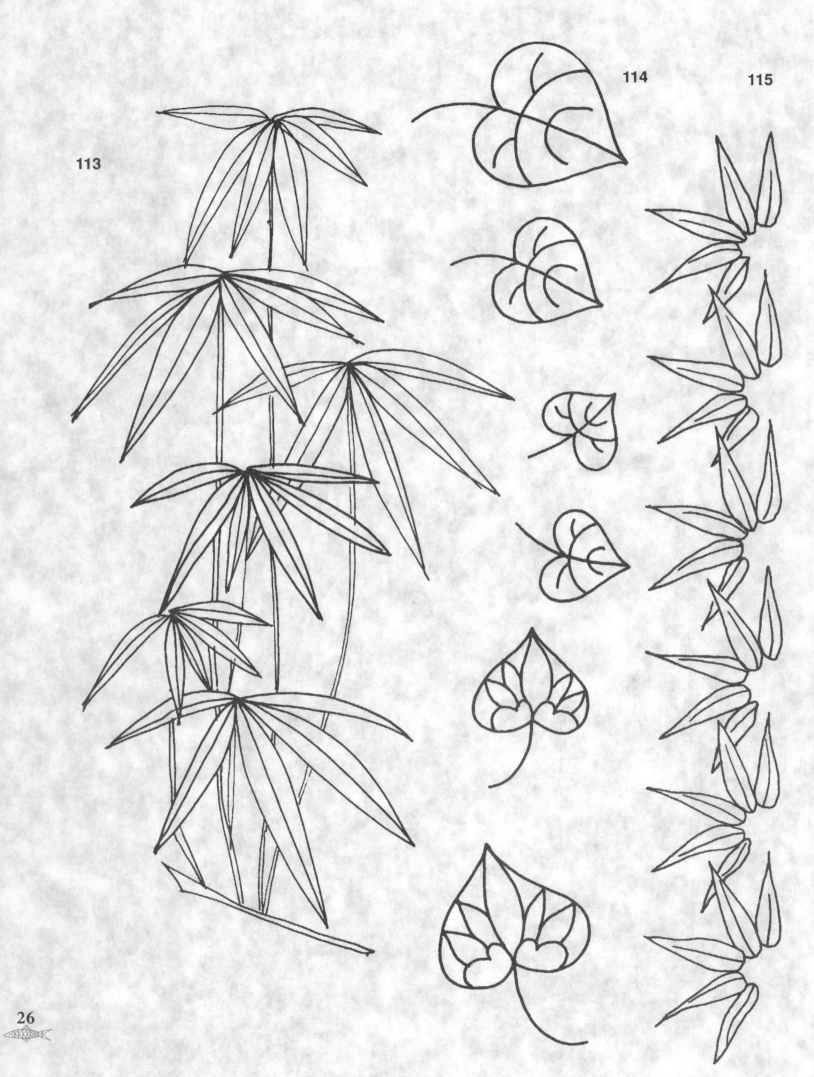

113

114

115

116

117

118

119

120

121

122

123

124

125

27

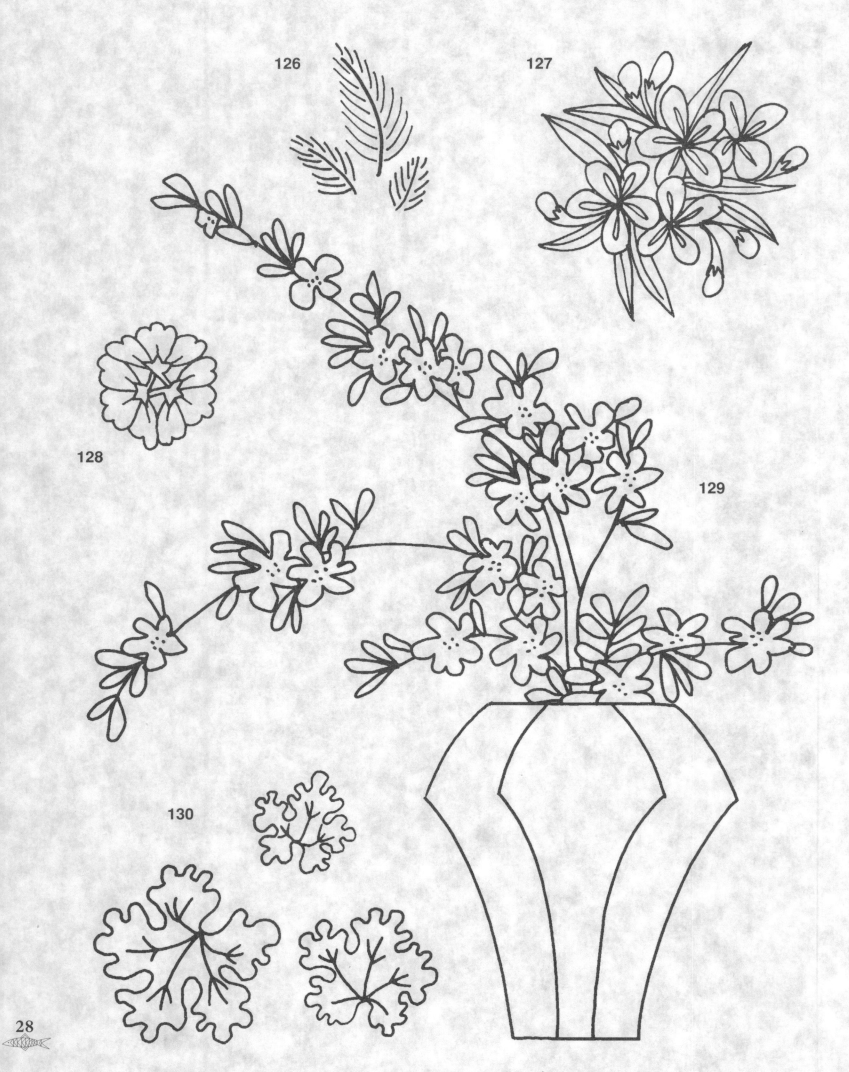

126

127

128

129

130

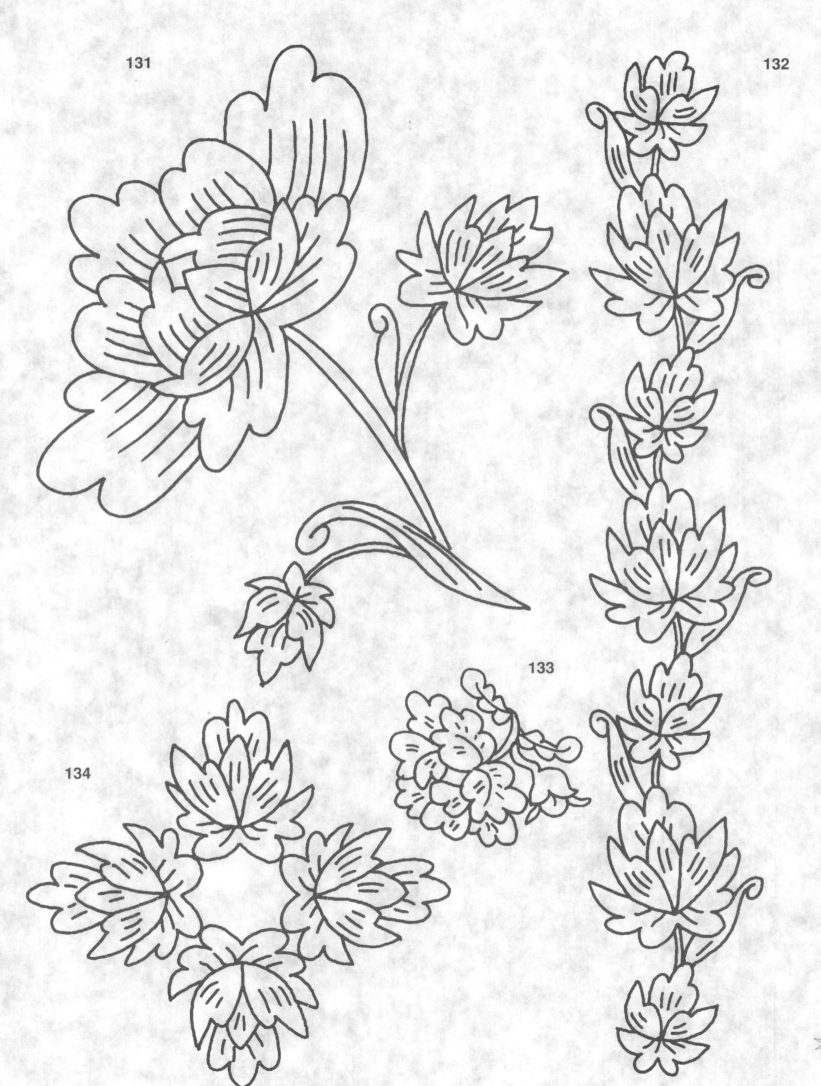

131

132

133

134

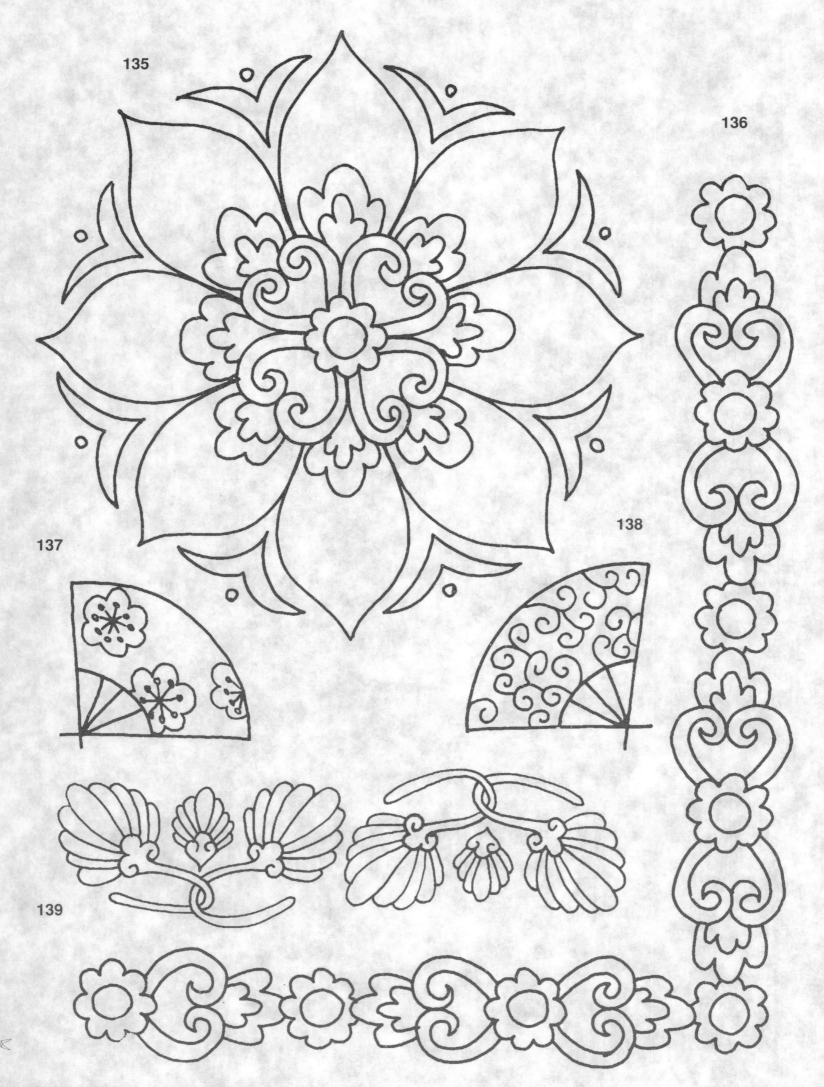

135

136

137

138

139

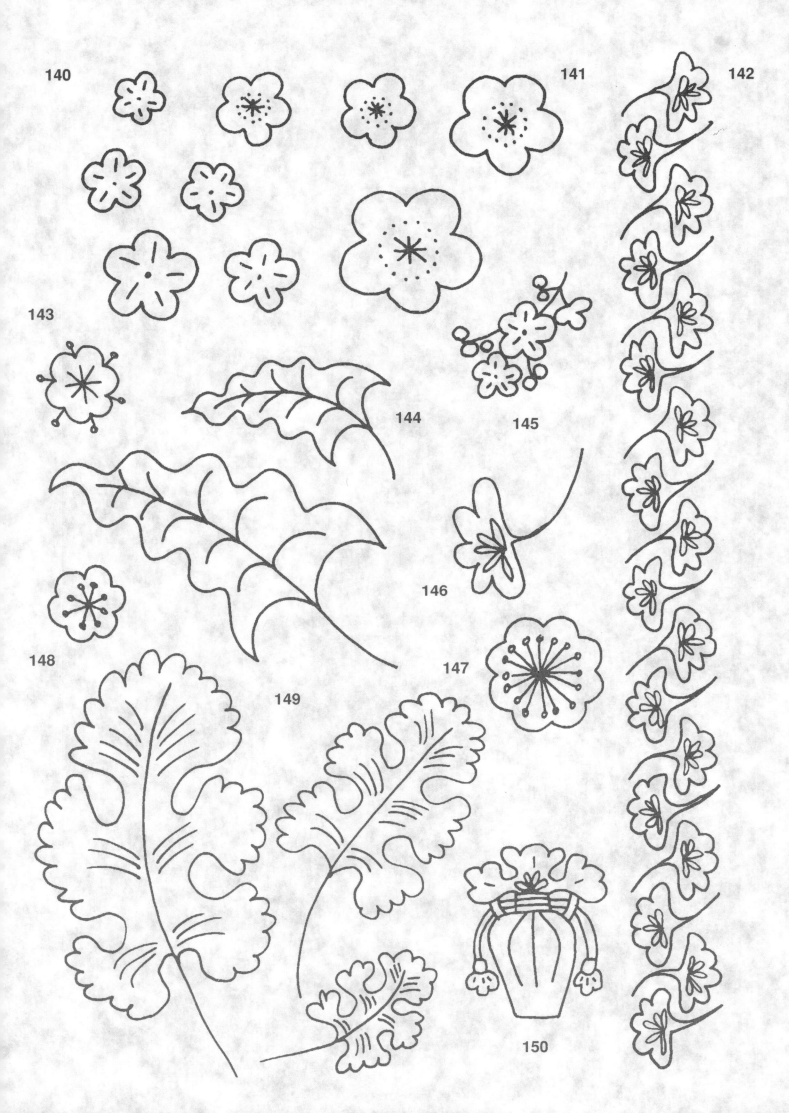

140

141

142

143

144

145

146

147

148

149

150

31

151

152

153

154

155

156

157

158

159

160

161

162

163

164

165

33

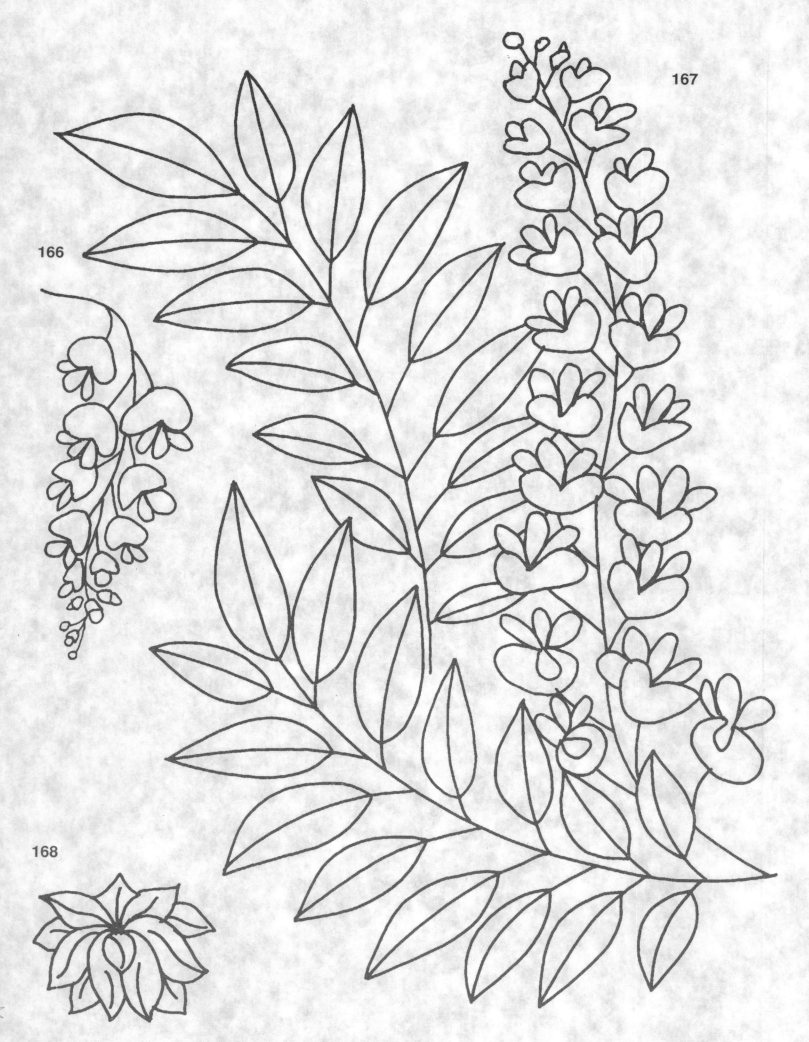

166

167

168

169

170

171

172

173

174

175

176

177

35

178

179

180

181

182

183

184

185

36

186

187

188

190

191

189

193

192

194

195

196

197

37

198

199

201

200

202

203

204

207

208

209

210

211

212

213

40

214

215

216

217

218

219

220

221

222

223

224

225

42

226

227

228

229

43

230

231

232

233

44

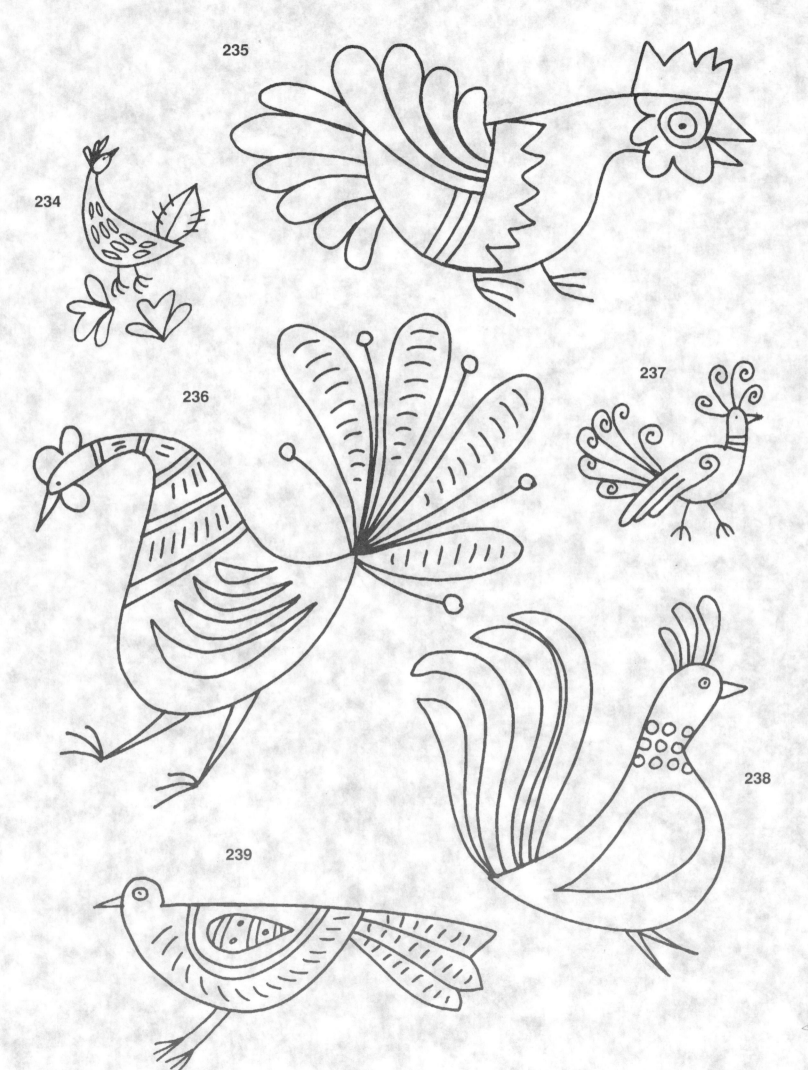

234

235

236

237

238

239

45

240

241

242

243

46

244

245

246

247

248

249

251

250

48

252

253

254

255

256

257

258

259

260 261 262 263

264

265

266

267

268

269

270

271

272

273

51

274

275

276

278

277

280

279

52

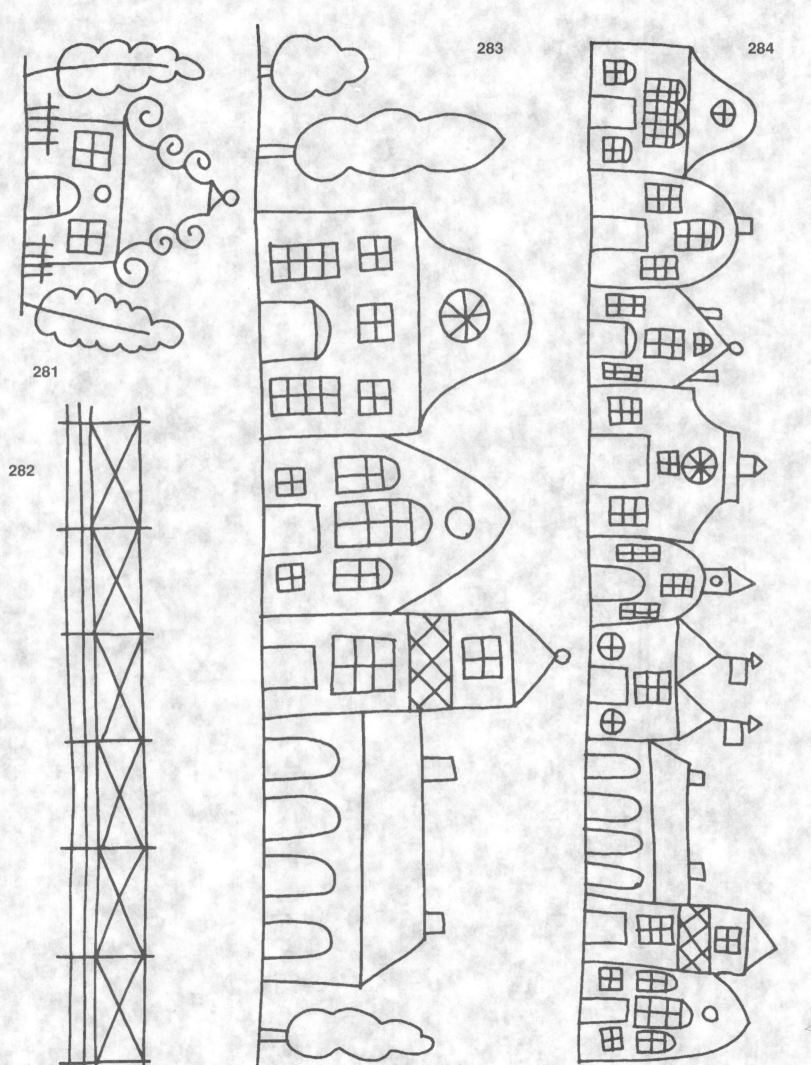

281

282

283

284

285

286

287

288

289

290

291

292

294

293

295

296

297

298

299

300

301

302

303

304

57

305

306

307

308

309

310

311

313

314

312

315

59

316

317

318

319

320

321

322

323

61

324

325

326

327

328

329

330   331   332

63

333

334

335

336

337

338

339

MORE EMBROIDERY PROJECTS

Doll

Transfer Page 40, No. 209 (Europe)

Stitches Chain stitch and satin stitch

DMC colours No. 598 (Light Turquoise); No. 704 (Ultra Light Christmas Green); No. 603 (Cerise); No. 823 (Dark Navy Blue); No. 725 (Topaz); No. 721 (Medium Orange Spice)

Vase

Transfer Page 41, No. 216 (Europe)

Stitches Chain stitch and satin stitch

DMC colours No. 939 (Very Dark Navy Blue); No. 800 (Light Delft Blue); No. 725 (Topaz); No. 820 (Very Dark Royal Blue); No. 798 (Dark Delft Blue)

Large heart

Transfer Page 39, No. 206 (Europe)

Stitches Chain stitch and satin stitch

DMC colours: No. 121 (Variegated Delft Blue)

Small heart

Transfer Page 52, No. 279 (Europe)

Stitches Chain stitch and satin stitch

DMC colours No. 725 (Topaz); No. 349 (Dark Peach); No. 319 (Very Dark Pistachio Green); No. 3348 (Light Yellow Green)

Flower circle

Transfer Page 57, No. 302 (India)

Stitches Chain stitch and satin stitch

DMC colours No. 333 (Very Dark Blue Violet); No. 704 (Ultra Light Christmas Green); No. 741 (Medium Tangerine)

PAINTING PROJECTS

Plates

Transfer Page 38, No. 228 (Europe)

~ Materials ~
Blank wooden plates
Acrylic paints *For the strawberry plate* – red, yellow, green and blue; *for the bird plate* – red, yellow, green and cream
Large and small paint brush
Furniture wax and soft cloth
Palette

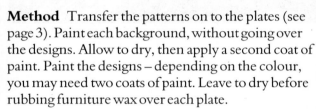

Method Transfer the patterns on to the plates (see page 3). Paint each background, without going over the designs. Allow to dry, then apply a second coat of paint. Paint the designs – depending on the colour, you may need two coats of paint. Leave to dry before rubbing furniture wax over each plate.

Bag

Transfer Page 54, No. 287 (India)

~ Materials ~
Canvas bag
White cotton fabric
Fabric paints: fuchsia, yellow, orange, green and black
Silver embroidery thread
Pearl beads
Needle
Small paintbrush
Plastic pipette
Glue stick

Method Transfer the design on to the white fabric. Paint all the coloured areas with a small brush. Allow to dry for approximately two hours. Decant a small amount of black paint into a pipette (see page 4) and then outline the design. Leave to dry for at least four hours then iron the fabric to fix the colours (see page 4). Turn under the edges of the fabric and then glue it to the front of the bag. Use silver thread and long stitches to secure the fabric firmly in place. Decorate further by sewing on pearl beads.

Tray

Transfer No. 204, page 38 (Europe)

~ Materials ~
Wooden tray
Acrylic paints: dark green, black, orange, russet brown, blue, pale green, dark green, cream, yellow, pale violet and dark violet
Large and small paintbrush
Palette
Coarse and fine grade sandpaper
Furniture wax and soft cloth

Method Paint the entire tray orange and allow to dry. Transfer the designs to the orange background. Apply a top coat of dark green, painting around the designs. Allow to dry for approximately two hours. Paint in the designs. Leave to dry, then distress the surface with sandpaper – start with a coarse grade and finish with a fine grade. Apply furniture wax all over the tray then polish off with a soft cloth.

Key cupboard

Transfer No. 101, page 23 (South America)

~ Materials ~
Wooden key cupboard
Acrylic paints: ultramarine blue, orange, yellow, red, dark blue, pale green, pink and cobalt blue
Large and small paintbrush
Palette
Coarse and fine grade sandpaper
Furniture wax and soft cloth

Method Paint the key cupboard red then allow to dry. Transfer the design on to the background. Apply a blue topcoat, painting around the design. Leave to dry for at least two hours, then apply a second coat if necessary and leave to dry. Paint the design and add free-painted borders to decorate the cupboard further. When completely dry, distress the surface by sanding first with coarse grade then with fine grade sandpaper. Apply furniture wax, then polish with a soft cloth.

Salt box

Transfer No. 272, page 51 (Europe)

~ Materials ~
Wooden salt box
Acrylic paints: yellow ochre, yellow,
orange, red and green
Large and small paintbrush
Furniture wax and soft cloth
Palette

Method Transfer the main flower head design on to the surface.
Paint the entire box green, leaving only the sunflower image
unpainted. Leave to dry for one hour before painting the
sunflower petals using yellow ochre and yellow and the centre
using orange and red. Add details in green. Allow to dry for
approximately one hour before waxing and polishing the box.

T-shirt

Transfers Nos. 1–48,
pages 9–14 (Oceania
and Africa)

~ Materials ~
White T-shirt
Pipette
Fabric paint: black

Method Transfer the designs on to a
white T-shirt. Decant black fabric paint
into a pipette (see page 4) and then use this
to outline the designs. Allow to dry for
approximately eight hours. Iron on the
reverse to fix the paint (see page 4).

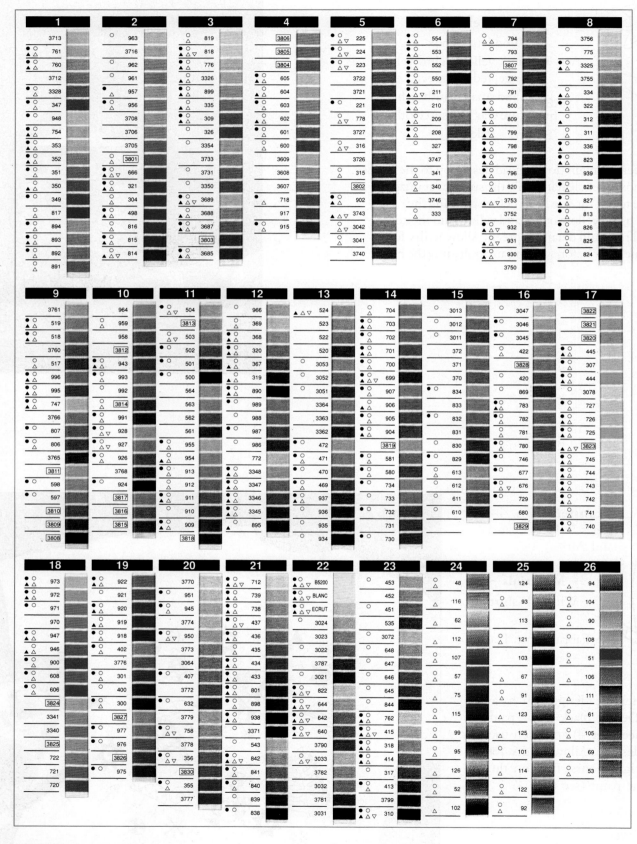

Stranded Cotton, D. 117
Pearl Cotton Art. 115 No. 3 ● No. 5 ○
Pearl Cotton Art. 116 No. 5 ▲ No. 8 △ No. 12 ▽

TABLEAU DE RECHERCHE DES COULEURS - KEY TO COLOUR NUMBERS

FARBTABELLE - TABEL OM KLEUREN UIT TE ZOEKEN - TABELLA RICERCA COLORI
TABLA PARA BUSCAR LOS COLORES - QUADRO DE PROCURA DAS CORES
FARVENUMMER OVERSIGT - FÄRGSÖKNINGSTABELL - TABELA KOLORÓW
颜色代号卡 - カラー番号表 - جدول تحديد الألوان

N°Couleur - Colour No - Farbnr. - Nr Kleur - N° colore - N° Color - N° Cor
Farve nr. - Färg nr. - Nr. koloru - 颜色代号 - カラー番号 - رقم اللون

Colonne - Column - Spalte - Kolom - Colonna - Columna - Coluna
Kolonne - Kolumn - Kolumna - 列 - 欄 - العمود

Couleur	Col	Couleur	Col	Couleur	Col	Couleur	Col	Couleur	Col	Couleur	Col	Couleur	Col	Couleur	Col	Couleur	Col	Couleur	Col
ECRUT	22	211	6	400	19	563	11	727	17	813	8	910	11	971	18	3347	12	3773	20
BLANC	22	221	5	402	19	564	11	729	16	814	2	911	11	972	18	3348	12	3774	20
B5200	22	223	5	407	20	580	14	730	14	815	2	912	11	973	18	3350	3	3776	19
48	24	224	5	413	23	581	14	731	14	816	2	913	11	975	19	3354	3	3777	20
51	26	225	5	414	23	597	9	732	14	817	1	915	4	976	19	3362	13	3778	20
52	24	300	19	415	23	598	9	733	14	818	3	917	4	977	19	3363	13	3779	20
53	26	301	19	420	16	600	4	734	14	819	3	918	19	986	12	3364	13	3781	22
57	24	304	2	422	16	601	4	738	21	820	7	919	19	987	12	3371	21	3782	22
61	26	307	17	433	21	602	4	739	21	822	22	920	19	988	12	3607	4	3787	22
62	24	309	3	434	21	603	4	740	17	823	8	921	19	989	12	3608	4	3790	22
67	25	310	23	435	21	604	4	741	17	824	8	922	19	991	10	3609	4	3799	23
69	26	311	8	436	21	605	4	742	17	825	8	924	10	992	10	3685	3	3801	2
75	24	312	8	437	21	606	18	743	17	826	8	926	10	993	10	3687	3	3802	5
90	26	315	5	444	17	608	18	744	17	827	8	927	10	995	9	3688	3	3803	3
91	25	316	5	445	17	610	15	745	17	828	8	928	10	996	9	3689	3	3804	4
92	25	317	23	451	23	611	15	746	16	829	15	930	7	3011	15	3705	2	3805	4
93	25	318	23	452	23	612	15	747	9	830	15	931	7	3012	15	3706	2	3806	4
94	26	319	12	453	23	613	15	754	1	831	15	932	7	3013	15	3708	2	3807	7
95	24	320	12	469	13	632	20	758	20	832	15	934	13	3021	22	3712	1	3808	9
99	24	321	2	470	13	640	22	760	1	833	15	935	13	3022	22	3713	1	3809	9
101	25	322	8	471	13	642	22	761	1	834	15	936	13	3023	22	3716	2	3810	9
102	24	326	3	472	13	644	22	762	23	838	21	937	13	3024	22	3721	5	3811	9
103	25	327	6	498	2	645	23	772	12	839	21	938	21	3031	22	3722	5	3812	10
104	26	333	6	500	11	646	23	775	8	840	21	939	8	3032	22	3726	5	3813	11
105	26	334	8	501	11	647	23	776	3	841	21	943	10	3033	22	3727	5	3814	10
106	26	335	3	502	11	648	23	778	5	842	21	945	20	3041	5	3731	3	3815	10
107	24	336	8	503	11	666	2	780	16	844	23	946	18	3042	5	3733	3	3816	10
108	26	340	6	504	11	676	16	781	16	869	16	947	18	3045	16	3740	5	3817	10
111	26	341	6	517	9	677	16	782	16	890	12	948	1	3046	16	3743	5	3818	11
112	24	347	1	518	9	680	16	783	16	891	1	950	20	3047	16	3746	6	3819	14
113	25	349	1	519	9	699	14	791	7	892	1	951	20	3051	13	3747	6	3820	17
114	25	350	1	520	13	700	14	792	7	893	1	954	11	3052	13	3750	7	3821	17
115	24	351	1	522	13	701	14	793	7	894	1	955	11	3053	13	3752	7	3822	17
116	24	352	1	523	13	702	14	794	7	895	12	956	2	3064	20	3753	7	3823	17
121	25	353	1	524	13	703	14	796	7	898	21	957	2	3072	23	3755	8	3824	18
122	25	355	20	535	23	704	14	797	7	899	3	958	10	3078	17	3756	8	3825	18
123	25	356	20	543	21	712	21	798	7	900	18	959	10	3325	8	3760	9	3826	19
124	25	367	12	550	6	718	4	799	7	902	5	961	2	3326	3	3761	9	3827	19
125	25	368	12	552	6	720	18	800	7	904	14	962	2	3328	1	3765	9	3828	16
126	24	369	12	553	6	721	18	801	21	905	14	963	2	3340	18	3766	9	3829	16
208	6	370	15	554	6	722	18	806	9	906	14	964	10	3341	18	3768	10	3830	20
209	6	371	15	561	11	725	17	807	9	907	14	966	12	3345	12	3770	20		
210	6	372	15	562	11	726	17	809	7	909	11	970	18	3346	12	3772	20		

Contents

First published in Great Britain 1999 by
Search Press Limited
Wellwood, North Farm Road,
Tunbridge Wells, Kent TN2 3DR

Reprinted 1999

Originally published in France 1998 by
Buchet/Chastel Pierre Zech Éditeur, Paris
Original title: *Transferts du Monde*
Copyright © Buchet/Chastel Pierre Zech Éditeur, Paris 1998

Photography: Charlie Abad

English translation by Norman Porter
English translation copyright © Search Press Limited 1999

ISBN 0 85532 896 7

Suppliers

If you have difficulty in obtaining any of the materials and equipment
mentioned in this book, then please write to the Publishers, at the address
above, for a current list of stockists, which includes firms who operate a
mail-order service.

Printed in Italy by Canale, Turin